I0815289

Granddaughter, I am so proud of the beautiful spirit I see in you. You have enriched my life in ways that are hard to describe... Your love will always be in my heart and mine in yours. The bond we have found is as everlasting as the spirit.

Titles by Marci
Published by
Blue Mountain Arts®

Friends Are Forever
A Gift of Inspirational
Thoughts to Thank You
for Being My Friend

To My Daughter
Love and Encouragement
to Carry with You on Your
Journey Through Life

To My Granddaughter
A Gift of Love and Wisdom
to Always Carry
in Your Heart

To My Sister
A Gift of Love and Inspiration
to Thank You
for Being My Sister

To My Son
Love and Encouragement
to Carry with You on Your
Journey Through Life

To My Granddaughter

A Gift of Love and Wisdom
to Always Carry
in Your Heart

Marci

Blue Mountain Press™
Boulder, Colorado

Library of Congress Control Number: 2014939961
ISBN: 978-1-68088-555-2 (previous ISBN: 978-1-59842-828-5)

Printed in China.
First printing of this edition: 2024

This book is printed on recycled paper.

This book is printed on paper that has been specially produced to be acid free (neutral pH) and contains no groundwood or unbleached pulp. It conforms with the requirements of the American National Standards Institute, Inc., so as to ensure that this book will last and be enjoyed by future generations.

Blue Mountain Arts, Inc.
P.O. Box 4549, Boulder, Colorado 80306

Contents

Dear Granddaughter...

You Are Hopes and Dreams About to Unfold

I am so happy to have you in my life... you are a gift I could have never foreseen. Your smile lights up the room as your twinkling eyes foretell a bright future... Your life is a scrapbook waiting to be filled with memories of love and family... You are a flower about to bloom... You are hopes and dreams and love made visible... You are my granddaughter, and I am so happy that you are a part of my life.

My Love
Is Always
...with you

You are always in my heart and never far from my thoughts, because on the day you were born, I promised to love you forever. My wish is that you find a place in the world that gives you a sense of contribution… that you find the kind of love that makes the stars shine brighter… and that you know the gift of gratitude that comes with living a life of compassion. Remember, wherever you are, whatever you do, wherever life takes you, I will always love you.

Watching You Grow Up...

Is One of My Greatest Joys

Having a granddaughter like you is a beautiful experience. It brings back so many memories as I remember a time when I was your age. As I think about the hopes and dreams I had growing up, I realize how quickly time passes. I wish I could stop the clock and keep you as you are… but life moves us always forward, and watching you grow up is one of my greatest joys. I'm thankful every day to see life carried through the generations and blossom in you.

My Life Is So Much Better

...Because of You

Being a grandparent has changed my life in ways that are hard to describe. The love I feel for you is stronger than I ever dreamed possible. I look at you and see the future about to unfold. I want so much for you to be happy... to understand the meaning of love... to know the satisfaction found in relationships. I am so proud as I see so many of those dreams fulfilled, and I'm grateful to have been touched by God's hand when He gave you to me as my granddaughter.

You Brighten My Life

I thought I had experienced all the best things in life, but when you were born I discovered a whole new world! You have given me so much joy and reminded me that the simplest things really do bring the most happiness! Your laugh always makes me smile, and each of your achievements warms my heart.

Some days we just need a hand to hold... Some days we just need a hug... Some days we just need a word of encouragement... Some days we just need someone to be there for a laugh and a memory... On my "some days" there is you! Thank you for all the good things you bring to my life.

You Put the "Grand"
Grandchildren Are a Blessing
...in Being a Grandparent

You have given me a second chance to enjoy that first smile... that first step... that first hug... that first laugh. Best of all, you have brought back sweet memories of my own first days of being a parent, allowing me to enjoy the journey all over again... this time with wiser eyes, a seasoned heart, and a perspective on life that is truly "grand!"

A
Granddaughter's
Love
...Is Forever

A granddaughter is a gift of hopes and dreams wrapped up in a beautiful life.

A granddaughter is an opportunity to reflect upon the past and a chance to see possibilities fulfilled.

A granddaughter carries hopes from the past and dreams of the future in her heart...

A granddaughter's path is hers to walk; a granddaughter's dreams are hers to create; a granddaughter's happiness is hers to define.

A granddaughter is understanding, kind, compassionate, caring, and giving.

A granddaughter reminds you of how much you are loved.

A granddaughter is a precious gift that is unwrapped a little bit each year.

A granddaughter shares the journey of life, celebrating love and joy and tears and hopes as only a woman can.

A granddaughter's love remains forever in your heart.

I Always
Wanted a
Granddaughter
...like you

I always wanted a granddaughter... someone to share wisdom and hope with... someone to love and encourage through life's challenges... someone to be proud of as I watched dreams be fulfilled and wishes come true. What a wonderful feeling to know I have what I always wanted... in you!

I've Learned
So Many
Important Lessons...
That I Want to
Share with You

Big problems can be solved in small steps.

When you are still, the gentle voice from within will guide you... listen carefully.

Remember to pray, and let God take the burden of worry from your heart.

Accept that we each learn life's lessons in our own way.

10 Simple Things to Remember

1. Love is why we are here.

2. The most important day is today.

3. If you always do your best, you will not have regrets.

4. In spite of your best efforts, some things are just out of your control.

5. Things will always look better tomorrow.

6. Sometimes a wrong turn will bring you to exactly the right place.

7. Sometimes when you think the answer is "no," it is just "not yet."

8. True friends share your joy, see the best in you, and support you through your challenges.

9. God and your parents will always love you.

10. For all your accomplishments, nothing will bring you more happiness than the love you find.

Hold On to Your Dreams...

Because Anything Is Possible

Your life holds for you endless possibilities. You have built a solid foundation, and you have worked hard for it. Continue to do what is necessary to move forward one day at a time. Write down your dreams and tuck them away, entrusting that all things will come at the right time. Keep sight always of what is important in life.

Remember that true happiness and purpose will be found in relationships – in the workplace and at home. Live each day open to guidance, and your purpose will be revealed to you...

Remember that you are special. There are talents locked away inside you just waiting for the right time to unfold.

Remember that dreams are the start of every great adventure. When you close your eyes and imagine your happy and successful self in the future, you are beginning your journey!

Remember that wisdom is a gift that comes with experience. Often, it is through our struggles that we gain the most understanding. We learn about who we are, what we believe, and what is really important through everyday living.

Remember to listen to your heart... it is where your courage lies. When you follow your heart, you may meet challenges, but each of your steps will be guided.

Always
Listen...
to Your Heart

Listen for that voice inside guiding you toward the right thing to do, the right path to travel, and the knowledge of what will bring you happiness and fulfillment. That voice is very quiet, like a whisper. Over time, and mostly through the challenges in life, you will learn to hear it more clearly. Whenever you feel that tug to do something new, help someone in need, or share what you have learned, listen carefully… and follow your heart toward your dreams.

Wisdom for Your Journey
FAITH
HOPE
LOVE
As You Follow Life's Path, Remember...

No matter where life takes you or what path you choose, you will always meet challenges. That is the way life is. There are no guarantees, and no matter how many things you do right or how many rules you follow, there will always be that fork in the road that makes you choose between this way or that. Whenever you meet this place, remember these things: You are loved... love will sustain you. You are strong... prayer will get you through anything. You are wise... the greatest gift of all lies within you.

Love Is
the Gift
Love is the
greatest gift
of all.
...I Most Want
You to Have

The one gift I most want you to have is the one that you ultimately must give yourself. It is knowing that everything you need to succeed in this life is right inside you. It is the joy that comes with the discovery of your God-given talents, which will come forth at just the right time. It is the belief that you can overcome all the challenges that come with navigating this journey of life. It is the realization that through whatever life hands you, you will always know that love is what matters after all.

I'm So Glad We're Family

Family means having someone to give you a hug when you need one.

Family means having someone to love you through good times and bad.

Family means having someone to share life's joys and to dry the tears through life's sorrows.

Family means that someone is there to shine a light on the path ahead... and shed some light on the path behind.

Families are special creations made up of people who love each other and are tied together with threads of common experience, memories, and values. You are such a special part of our family.

You Are a...
Shining Star

You've had a special light around you from the day you were born... It shines brightly and makes you stand out in a crowd. Your heart is always open, ready to share or just listen to those in need. Your arms are always ready with a hug and a reminder that God has a plan. Thank you for the inspiration you are and for the bright light that shines as you. You are a shining star!

Give Yourself
a Hug Today
...from Me!

I want you to always remember what you mean to me. The joys we have shared and the memories we have made through our lives are a gift beyond measure. Thank you for your love. Today, consider yourself hugged!

I Hope
You Know...
I'd Do Anything
for You

No matter what is happening
in your life, remember...
I'm here for you...
I will always love you...
I'll stand by you...
I'll encourage you to remain hopeful
no matter how hard life gets and
until the light is shining again!
I'll remind you to hang in there
because a lot of people love you more
than words can say!

You Are
Always in...
My Prayers

You are always in my prayers, and I want you to remember that so you will be open to the grace that comes your way. I have asked that you feel the love of God like a gentle breeze when you need inspiration... that your faith remain unwavering through all of life's challenges... and that hope be the burning light that always guides your way.

Everything Happens
This Way Home
...for a Reason

So often we wonder about the "whys" in life… "Why did this happen?" "Why me?" "Why now?" But there is a secret that wise men know… Bumps in the road are an inevitable part of life that soften us, make us grow, and bestow upon us the virtue of compassion. Often it is only with the passing of time that it becomes clear that the cloud really did have a silver lining, and now we have wisdom, strength, and hope to share. And at last, we understand the true meaning of the phrase "Everything happens for a reason."

On the Days When Things Get Difficult...

Remember it is perseverance that will get you through. Give thanks for the talent that has set you on your path... for the inner strength that has helped you navigate the obstacles... and for the faith that has carried you through the most difficult of days.

And don't forget to ask for help when you most need it. It's easy to get caught up in whatever is happening and not realize that help is always available just for the asking. That help is called "grace." It is always abundant... always accessible... and always exactly what we need.

You Are Stronger...
FAITH
HOPE
LOVE
Than You May Realize

There are times in our lives when we face a hardship that we do not think we can bear. We try but cannot make sense of it all. After much struggle, we seek that place called "acceptance" and reach out to others who understand what we have been through.

It is then, as we share our wisdom, strength, and hope, that we get a small glimpse of a larger plan... one that shows us that love blesses the giver and the receiver and allows us to see how strong we really are. I know your inner strength and faith in God will carry you through these times and into the light again.

When You Need Encouragement, Remember These Things...

Life's inevitable adversities call forth our courage.

You have a lot of wisdom inside you.

God's plan will unfold with perfect timing.

The voice of your soul will lead the way.

...and Then Say This Prayer

Guardian angel, light my way.
Please be with me through the day.
Remind me I am in your care
and should help be needed,
you will be there.

Cultivate Your
Unique Talents...
Believe
and Let Your
Inner Light
Shine

Success is an opportunity to recognize our talents and strengths, remembering that these are both a gift and a responsibility. When you work hard and accept life's ups and downs one day at a time, you will be rewarded with the experience of "who you are."

There's a Right Time for Everything

If you are stuck in thinking and can't find a solution, switch gears to physical activity. Sometimes the answer will just pop into your head.

Take some time for quiet reading and reflection in the morning – your mind is very open then.

If you're trying to figure out something, don't force the solution. Clean out a closet or a drawer instead – live a metaphor.

When growing up, we often hear the words, "Don't just sit there – do something!" Often the exact opposite is called for.

Confusion can be a gift. It keeps us from moving forward until we have clarity. There's a right time for everything.

I Love
You
...and I
Believe in You

There have never been words
more powerful than
"I love you"...
or more meaningful than
"Thank you"...
or more sustaining than
"I believe in you"...
So I'm saying these things
to you now:
"I love you more
than words can say.
I am so thankful
you are a part of my life.
And no matter what,
I will always believe in you!"

You Can Make a Difference...
Just by Being You

Live your beliefs... and be a powerful example of love in the world.

Be compassionate... Life is difficult, and people are often working through private battles.

Demonstrate acts of kindness... "Little ones" are watching you and learning about compassion.

Encourage someone today... The words "everything will be okay" can lighten the heart of another. Share love... there is an endless supply.

Be hopeful... Your attitude will uplift the spirit of another.

When Good Things Come into Your Life...
Love always returns to renew the spirit.
Remember to Pass Them On!

We each have a chance to brighten the day of another. It can be a kind smile... a simple hello... shared inspiration... or an unexpected gesture to let someone know that their being in the world makes a difference. When good things come into your life, I hope you'll be inspired to brighten the day of another.

Celebrate
Life...
Faith Will Light
Your Path

Every day is a gift and a reason to celebrate when we remember to be grateful for the things that are really important. Life brings us joys and sorrows, struggles and triumphs, but it is our simple blessings that will get us through. Faith will light your path, hope will keep you strong, love will bring you your greatest joys, and your friendships will remind you that every day is a reason to celebrate.

Believe in Miracles...

Angels Are Everywhere!

Sometimes we feel that we are all alone, as life brings us challenges to overcome and hardships to bear. But when we least expect it, help can appear. It may be a kind word from a stranger or a phone call at just the right time, and we are suddenly surrounded with the loving grace of God. Miracles happen every day because angels are everywhere.

Think of Each Day

Hope

...as a New Start

Sometimes we make mistakes... that is a part of our nature. We fall down because we are human and imperfect. Fortunately, each day is a chance to begin again, to wipe the slate clean, and to remember that today is the only day that exists. The past is gone... tomorrow is in the future... but today is a chance for a new start!

Wherever You
Go in Life,
Granddaughter...
Believe
Take These Thoughts
with You

Wherever life takes you, always take this knowledge along. It will get you through difficult times and answer many of the questions that you will have about life.

Real and lasting beauty is found inside you.

True happiness is found with friends and family.

Your purpose in life will call you at just the right time.

The Road of Life
If All Else fails Pet the Dog
All Paths Lead to Home
...Has Many Turns

Sometimes the road of life takes us to a place we had planned... Sometimes it shows us a surprise around the bend we could never have anticipated. We make decisions based on the information we have... We accept the ups and downs as they come... We live "one day at a time." But often we find it is only when we look back that we can see that what we had thought was a "wrong turn" has brought us to exactly the right place and every step was a right one after all!

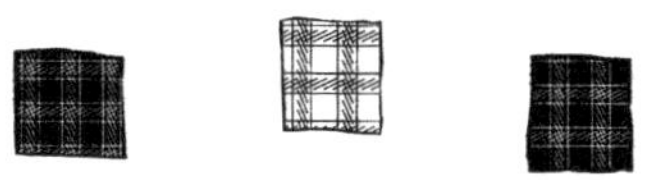

No Matter How Busy Life Gets...

You Are Always in My Heart

In today's world, life gets so busy that the days roll by and we realize we have not spoken to the ones we love! I want you to know that you are always in my heart... You are one of the most important people in my life, and even if we do not speak every day, my best thoughts and wishes are always with you.

I Pray
for Your
Guardian Angel
...to Stay by
Your Side

I pray for you every day and ask your guardian angel to stay by your side… to bring you inspiration when life gets you down… to fill your heart with determination when life puts obstacles in your path… and to shower you with grace to nurture your spiritual growth as you travel your path through life. May your angel wrap you in God's love every day!

These Are the Things
Peace
Joy
Love
Hope
Faith
I Wish for You

I wish you a life filled with love… A true love to share your every dream… Family love to warm your heart… And priceless love found in the gift of friendship.

I wish you peace… Peace in knowing who you are… Peace in knowing what you believe in… And peace in the understanding of what is important in life…

I wish you joy... Joy as you awaken each day with gratitude in your heart for new beginnings... Joy when you surrender to the beauty of a flower or a baby's smile... And joy, a hundred times returned, for each time you've brought happiness to another's heart.

I wish you hope... Hope is a gift from God. It is a state of mind in which you remember that your needs are always taken care of and that miracles are before you every day.

I wish you faith... Faith is the assurance of things not seen. It is knowing that God is always by your side through all of life's journey and guiding your steps every day.

If you have these things, whatever challenges life brings, you will get through.

Love Is the Gift I Receive Every Day...

Because You Are My Granddaughter

You have given me so much to be thankful for as I watch you move through life and develop all the qualities that make you so beautiful. Your shining spirit fills my heart and makes me so thankful for the beautiful gift of you!

May God
Bless You...
and Keep You

On the days when you need inspiration, I pray you are blessed with these understandings and that you always keep them in your heart.

You are one of God's perfect creations, and you have everything you need to fulfill your life's purpose.

You are never alone... on the day when you need it most, an angel will send a message of hope.

You are goodness and light, and when you share that part of yourself, you will discover pure joy.

With All My Heart...

I Love You

With all my heart, I love you and wish you the very best that life can bring.

With all my soul, I pray for you and ask that your guardian angel always keep you safe and inspired.

With all my being, I hope that you always know you are loved, that you always remember you are a child of God, and that in the deepest part of your being, you know my love will be with you wherever you go.

Granddaughter...

I Couldn't Be More Proud of You

Today and always, know how proud I am of you. You are cultivating your unique talents and letting your "inner light" shine. When I look at you and how you've grown, I feel so happy! It's not just the beauty in your face but your shining spirit that lights up my world! I don't know where the time has gone... or when yesterday became today... but each time I think of the joy you are in my life, I know I am blessed to have you as my granddaughter.

About Marci

Marci began her career by hand painting floral designs on clothing. No one was more surprised than she was when one day, in a single burst of inspiration and a completely new and different art style, her delightful characters sprang from her pen! "Their wild and crazy hair is a sign of strength," she thought, "and their crooked little smiles are endearing." She quickly identified the charming characters as Mother, Daughter, Sister, Father, Son, Friend, and so on until all the people and places in life were filled. Then, with her own loved ones in mind, she wrote a true and special sentiment to each one. This would be the beginning of a wonderful success story, which today still finds Marci writing each and every one of her verses in this same personal way.

Marci is a self-taught artist who has always enjoyed writing and art. She is thrilled to see how her delightful characters and universal messages of love have touched the hearts and lives of people everywhere. Her distinctive designs can also be found on Blue Mountain Arts greeting cards, calendars, bookmarks, and other gift items.

To learn more about Marci, look for Children of the Inner Light on Facebook or visit her website: www.MARCIonline.com.